F VW
RECIPES

Compiled by
Simon Haseltine

*Illustrated with
nostalgic photographs*

Index

All recipes serve 2 unless otherwise stated

These classic retro images of campervans in this book have been selected from brochures collected by
Volkswagen author and enthusiast Richard Copping. His works include "VW Transporter – the first 60 years",
an impressive book designed to celebrate the 60th anniversary of the launch of the vehicle in 1949.
Printed & published by Dorrigo, Manchester, England © Copyright

Camper Van Chicken Risotto

A very quick and totally scrummy risotto for a warm Mediterranean summer's evening – wherever you are!

2 free range chicken breasts (chopped)
Handful mushrooms (sliced)
1 small onion (chopped)
1 small red pepper (cubed)
1 chicken stock cube
1 pack quick-cook rice (flavoured, 5 minute variety)
Water (in accordance with packet rice instructions)

Fry the onion for around 5 minutes until soft, then add the chicken and stir-fry for a few more minutes until brown. Add the pepper and mushrooms and gently fry for 5 more minutes. Add the crumbled stock cube, packet rice and water and simmer for 5 minutes (or in accordance with pack instructions) until all the water has been absorbed and the rice is cooked. Serve with some chunky bread and a large glass of red wine.

Moroccan Meatballs

A combination of international flavours brought to your camper van...

1 pack Swedish meatballs (in the chiller in most supermarkets)
1 onion (chopped)   2 cloves garlic (chopped)
Handful dried apricots (chopped)
Tin chopped tomatoes   1 oz. flaked almonds
Handful coriander leaves   Mixed herbs

Fry the onion for 5 minutes until soft, then add the garlic, mixed herbs, almonds and apricots and stir for a few more minutes. Add the chopped tomatoes (with all the juice) and the meatballs and simmer for 10 minutes until heated through. Fold in the coriander and serve with some chunky bread.

Coastal Fish Curry

If you are travelling along the coast, visit a local fish market
and buy some freshly caught fish...

8oz of fresh white fish – ask for a selection of off-cuts. (chunked)
1 onion (chopped)   2 garlic cloves (chopped)
1 tablespoon curry powder (or to taste)
1 large can chopped tomatoes
Vegetable stock cube
3 fl. oz. water
4 oz. rice to serve

Cook the rice in accordance with the pack instructions. Meanwhile, fry the onion
for around 5 minutes until soft, then add the garlic and curry powder and stir for a
few more minutes. Next, add the tomatoes and crumbled stock cube and water and
bring to the boil. Simmer for a couple of minutes, then add the fish. Cook gently
for 5 minutes and serve on a bed of rice.

Vegetarian Chilli

Spice up your cooking and warm up your evenings with this light and tasty chilli...

1 onion (chunked)
4 garlic cloves (chopped)
1 red chilli (diced – with seeds if you like it hot)
4 button mushrooms (chopped)
Tin chopped tomatoes
Small tin kidney beans
Handful green beans (halved)
4 fl. oz. water
Hot chilli sauce
Crème fraiche and chunky bread to serve

Fry the onion, garlic, mushrooms and chilli for 5 minutes. Then add the remaining ingredients and simmer for 10 minutes. Stir in some chilli sauce to taste and serve topped with a dollop of crème fraiche and chunky bread on the side.

Boozy Garlic Sausage and Herby Pasta

A quick and easy dish to cook on a warm pleasant evening...

3 oz. dried pasta
Large red onion (sliced)
Selection mushrooms (large handful – sliced)
Tin chopped tomatoes
Dried mixed herbs (good pinch)
4 cloves garlic (crushed)
Garlic smoked sausage (thinly sliced)
Red wine (a good glug)
Oats (a good pinch)

Place pasta in some water, bring to the boil and cook until tender in accordance with pack instructions. Meanwhile, fry the onion for a few minutes until softened, add the garlic, a good pinch of herbs, mushrooms and sausage and fry for around 5 minutes until brown. Add the chopped tomatoes, wine and oats, stir and simmer for a few more minutes until cooked through. Drain the cooked pasta and fold in the mixture. Serve with some locally baked crusty bread and the rest of the wine...

Crabby Cromer Fish Cakes

Wonderful if you are parked up on the Norfolk coast and can buy local Cromer crab...

2 tbsp diced red pepper	1 egg
1 small onion (finely chopped)	Pinch dried mixed herbs
14 oz. mashed potato	1 tbsp mustard
10 oz. fresh or tinned crabmeat	Half cup breadcrumbs

Fry the pepper and onion for a few minutes until soft. In a bowl, add the onion mixture to the crabmeat, egg, herbs, mustard and mashed potato, seasoning with salt and pepper. Roll the crabmeat mixture into golf ball size balls and roll in the breadcrumbs. Press down to form cakes. Fry the crab cakes over a moderate heat until golden and serve with a colourful salad.

Market Garden Vegetable Curry

Any selection of fresh vegetables will make this delicious curry dish...

1 onion (chopped)	4 button mushrooms (sliced)
1 potato (cubed)	Vegetable stock cube
1 courgette (halved and sliced)	Tin chopped tomatoes
1 carrot (halved and sliced)	2 tablespoons curry powder (or to taste)

Fresh coriander (small handful)
Rice and naan bread to serve

Fry the onion for around 5 minutes until soft. Then add all the remaining vegetables, curry powder and stock cube (but not the tinned tomatoes) and stir for a few more minutes. Add the tinned tomatoes and juice and simmer until the vegetables are tender, adding a little additional water if required. Fold in a small handful of fresh coriander and serve over rice with naan bread.

Cheeky Chinese Chicken

A cheeky Chinese dish, cooked in a flash...

2 chicken breasts (thinly sliced)
1 onion (chopped)
1 small red pepper (thinly sliced)
Handful mushrooms (sliced)
1 jar Chinese sauce
1 chicken stock cube
Quick cook noodles to serve

Fry the onion for around 5 minutes until soft. Add the chicken and stock cube and quickly cook until brown all over. Add the red pepper and mushrooms and stir-fry for a few more minutes, then add the sauce and simmer for 10 minutes. Meanwhile, cook the noodles in accordance with packet instructions. Fold the noodles into the chicken and serve – with chopsticks, of course!

Camper Chilli Con Carne

The 4 Cs of camper cuisine...

8 oz. minced beef	Tin chopped tomatoes
1 large onion (chopped)	Teaspoon dried chilli
4 cloves garlic (crushed)	Hot chilli sauce (to taste)
Handful mushrooms (sliced)	Beef stock cube

Rice and pitta bread to serve

Fry the onion, chilli and garlic for around 5 minutes until soft, then add the mince and crumbled stock cube and fry until brown. Add the mushrooms and cook for a few more minutes, then the tomatoes and simmer gently for 30 minutes. Taste and add your favourite chilli sauce to taste. Meanwhile, cook the rice in accordance with packet instructions. Serve the chilli over the rice, together with pitta bread to mop up the juices.

Buttery Potato and Broccoli Mash

Serve with the Sausage and Bean stew for a warming evening's supper...

4 potatoes
1 clump of broccoli (just the florets required)
Knob of butter
A little milk

Boil the potatoes and broccoli (add the broccoli after 10 minutes) in the same pan until tender, then drain and mash with a little milk and the butter. Season to taste and serve with a sausage and bean stew.

Saucy Sausage and Bean Stew

Easy to make, delicious to eat...

4 Sausages (cooked and sliced)	14 oz. can chopped tomatoes
1 onion (chopped)	1 garlic clove, finely chopped
14 oz. can baked beans	Small can sweetcorn, drained

A touch of hot chilli sauce

Fry the onion for 5 minutes until soft, then add the sausages and garlic for a further minute or two. Add the beans, tomatoes, chilli sauce and sweetcorn and simmer for around 10 minutes to reduce the liquid. Season and serve with delicious buttery Potato and Broccoli mash.

Mexican V-Wraps

A perfect, spicy supper for a lazy, balmy evening...

1 red onion (chopped)
1 breast of chicken (thinly sliced)
Half red pepper (thinly sliced)
2 large open cup mushrooms (thinly sliced)
Tin chopped tomatoes
Pack Mexican Spices or 1 teaspoon Chilli Powder
Hot Chilli Sauce   Pack Mexican Wraps
Greek Yogurt   Salad

Fry the onion for a few minutes until soft, then add the sliced chicken and brown all over. Add the red pepper, mushroom and spices and fry for around 5 minutes. Add around half the chopped tomatoes and simmer for 10 minutes, adding more chopped tomatoes as required if the mixture gets too dry. Add further chilli sauce to taste. Serve by spooning spicy chicken onto each wrap, top with a spoonful of cooling Greek Yogurt, close and eat with a crunchy side salad and a large glass of chilled white wine.

Crumbly Cheesey Mushrooms

Buy some local crumbly cheese and enjoy this delicious dish...

4 large flat field mushrooms (2 each)
Half cup of strong local cheese (crumbled)
Small handful of walnuts (chopped)
Knob of butter

Gently fry the mushrooms both sides in the butter until tender. Add the cheese and walnuts to the top and either heat under a grill or place a lid over the frying pan to melt the cheese. Serve on a bed of salad leaves for lunch or with a poached egg for breakfast.

Local Trout with a Red Wine Sauce

A wonderful combination of flavours, especially if you can find some locally caught trout on your travels...

2 medium size trout (gutted) (or 2 large sardines/pilchards)
4 oz. pancetta
12 fl. oz. red wine
1 tbsp sugar

Place the trout on the BBQ and cook each side for around 5 minutes. In a pan, fry the pancetta for around 4 minutes, then add the red wine and sugar. Bring to the boil and simmer gently for 5 minutes or until the sauce has thickened. Drizzle the sauce over the trout and serve with a crispy green salad.

Barbecue Sausages

These sausages wrapped in smoked bacon and cheese with a
barbeque sauce are a favourite with children.

1 lb. large pork and beef sausages
8 slices processed cheese
8 rashers smoked back bacon (derinded)

SAUCE
1 tablespoon vegetable oil   1 onion, peeled   1 oz. brown sugar
2 teaspoons English mustard   2 tablespoons Worcestershire sauce
14 oz. tin chopped tomatoes   1 tablespoon parsley, chopped
Salt and pepper

Grill sausages until browned and leave to cool a little. Place cheese slices on
bacon rashers and roll around sausages, one per sausage. Secure with cocktail
sticks and return to grill for approximately 10 minutes, turning occasionally, until
bacon is cooked. To make sauce, heat oil in saucepan, add onion and sauté until
softened. Stir in the sugar, mustard, Worcestershire sauce, tomatoes, parsley and
seasoning. Bring to the boil and simmer for 5 minutes. Transfer to a serving bowl
and serve with sausages. Serves 4.

Beefy Pasta Bolognaise

Far less messy to eat than traditional Spaghetti Bolognaise, in a confined place...!

6 oz. mince meat	1 Beef stock cube
1 onion (chopped)	2 cloves garlic (chopped)
Handful mushrooms (thinly sliced)	Pinch mixed herbs
Tin chopped tomatoes	Oil

6 oz. pasta

Fry the onion in oil in a frying pan for 5 minutes until soft. Add the mince and brown, then drain off any excess oil. Stir in the mushrooms, garlic, mixed herbs and stock cube for a few moments and then add the chopped tomatoes. Simmer for 30 minutes until sauce has reduced. Meanwhile, cook the pasta according to the pack instructions. Drain the pasta and fold in the Bolognaise sauce. Serve with chunks of olive bread.

Veggie Tonight

A delicious vegetarian meal all can enjoy...

4 large tomatoes (quartered)
Pesto (to taste but 2 tablespoons works well)
2 tablespoons crème fraiche
Dash hot chilli sauce
1 packet quick cook spinach and ricotta filled ravioli
Olive oil
Salad to serve

Fry the tomatoes in the oil for a few minutes, then fold in the pesto, chilli sauce and crème fraiche and warm through. Meanwhile, cook the ravioli in accordance with the pack instructions, drain and fold into the tomato mixture. Serve with a colourful salad.

Camper Chicken Fricassee

Try this one pot version of a classic dish...

2 legs of chicken	4 button mushrooms (quartered)
2 cloves of garlic (chopped)	½ pint water
1 large onion (chopped)	1 chicken stock cube
1 small red pepper (sliced)	Pinch mixed herbs
1 carrot (sliced)	Ground pepper

Quick-cook rice to serve

Place the chicken on the BBQ or in a separate pan until cooked through. Meanwhile, fry the onion for 5 minutes until soft, then add the garlic, pepper, carrot, mushrooms and herbs and stir-fry for a further 5 minutes. Add the stock cube and water and simmer for 20 minutes or until the vegetables are tender. Season well with black pepper. Add the cooked chicken legs for the last 5 minutes of cooking and serve with rice.

West Indian Corned Beef Hash

A recipe from a VW Camper Van friend – tried and tested...

1 onion	1 tin Corned Beef (diced)
4 cloves of garlic (crushed)	Tin chopped tomatoes
Dried mixed herbs	Hot chilli sauce

4 oz. rice

Chop the onion and fry for a few minutes until starting to brown. Add a pinch of mixed herbs and the garlic, stir, then add the diced corned beef and fry for a few more minutes. Add the chopped tomatoes and hot chilli sauce (to taste) and simmer for 10 minutes. Meanwhile, cook the rice, drain and fold into the hash mix. Serve under the stars with a large glass of red wine.

Barmy Beetroot and Watercress Salad

Ideal, as you can buy cooked beetroot packed in vacuum packs
which needs no refrigeration...

Handful watercress
Packet cooked beetroot (4 beets, cubed)
2 free range eggs (or 2 each if really hungry)
2 tsp mustard (wholegrain works well)
Dash vinegar
2 tsp sugar
4 fl. oz. olive oil
Salt and ground black pepper

For the dressing, place the mustard, sugar and vinegar into a bowl and whisk together. Gradually add the oil, whisking continuously, until the dressing thickens, then season with salt and freshly ground black pepper. Add the beetroot and fold together. Meanwhile, poach the eggs. To serve, scatter the watercress onto the plates and spoon over the beetroot dressing, then place the poached egg(s) on top.

Beef Stew in Red Wine

Wherever you are, buy some local beef from the farmer's market and enjoy this one-pot meal, with plenty of wine left over for the cook...

2 x 6 oz. rump steaks (cubed)   **Pinch mixed herbs**
1 large onion (sliced)   **2 glasses red wine**
2 cloves of garlic (chopped)   **1 can chopped tomatoes**
New potatoes to serve

In a little oil, fry the steak for 2 minutes to brown on both sides. Remove from the pan and then fry the onion, garlic and herbs in the remaining juices for 5 further minutes. Add the tomatoes and wine to the pan and simmer for 10 minutes until the sauce has thickened. Return the steak and simmer for a further 2 minutes and serve with some local new potatoes.

Camper Van Burgers

Your own van-made beefburgers...

6 oz. minced beef
1 large onion (finely chopped)
Pinch mixed herbs
1 egg
Rolls and extra fried onions to serve

Add the beef to most of the onions, herbs and egg and mix well. Divide into 4 balls and squash down to form burgers. Fry both sides unto brown and cooked through. Serve in the rolls with extra fried onions and hot English mustard on the side.

Scrummy Sweetcorn with Spicy Chutney

Get the BBQ out and enjoy this lunchtime dish...

2 corn cobs	**Large pinch dried chilli flakes**
2 tomatoes (chopped)	**Salt and black pepper**
2 tsp tomato purée	**Olive oil**
2 tsp clear honey	**Knob of butter**

Place the chopped tomatoes, tomato purée, honey and chilli flakes into a small pan, add a little water and season to taste, then simmer for around 10 minutes until reduced to a chutney consistency. Meanwhile, light the BBQ and chargrill the sweetcorn (wrapped in its own leaves or with foil and a knob of butter), for around 10 minutes, turning occasionally, until golden and cooked. Serve the chutney over the sweetcorn and enjoy with a glass of wine....

Posh Salmon Supper

For that special occasion whilst on the road...

4 slices smoked salmon   **2 small free range eggs**
8 asparagus spears   **Olive oil**
Freshly ground black pepper

Add a little oil to a frying pan and heat. Add the asparagus spears and fry for 3 minutes until browned on all sides. Add the smoked salmon and cook for one minute. Remove and keep warm. Fry the eggs in the remaining oil. Lay the asparagus onto a serving plate, place the salmon on top, then top with the eggs and season with black pepper. Serve with a glass of fizzy champagne...

Peri Peri Chicken

A tasty Camper Van version of this spicy dish...

4 free range chicken drumsticks
1 small red chilli (finely chopped – seeds removed)
1 small green chilli (finely chopped – seeds removed)
1 tablespoon balsamic vinegar
Pinch mixed herbs   2 cloves garlic
1 lemon (halved)   1 teaspoon local honey

Slash the chicken with a sharp knife and place in a bowl. Mix together the chillies, balsamic vinegar, mixed herbs, garlic, lemon juice from half the lemon and honey and pour over the chicken. Marinade for 30 minutes. Wrap the chicken drumsticks in foil (2 in each parcel), ensuring the marinade is evenly distributed, and place over the BBQ. Cook for 15 to 20 minutes, turning a few times, or until chicken juices run clear. Serve with the other half of lemon, crusty bread and a colourful salad.

Vegetarian Shepherd's Pie

Served without the shepherd, of course...

1 small onion (chopped)   1 carrot (finely chopped)
Can chopped tomatoes   Handful mushrooms (finely sliced)
Pinch mixed herbs   Pinch oats   Vegetable stock cube
Small can lentils   Glass red wine
1 lb. sweet potato (cut into chunks)
1 knob of butter   Grated cheese
Green beans to serve (tinned or fresh)

Fry the onion for around 5 minutes until soft, then stir in the mushrooms, carrots, oats and herbs. Add the wine and crumbled stock cube and simmer for 10 minutes. Add the lentils and canned tomatoes and simmer for a further 10 minutes until reduced and cooked through. Meanwhile, cook the sweet potato until tender (around 15 minutes on the boil), drain and mash with some butter. Place the lentil mixture into a dish, spoon over the sweet potato and grate cheese on top. If you have a grill, then brown the top, otherwise serve immediately in the dish with some green beans.

Butternut Squash and Herby Risotto

A light and creamy dish for a balmy summer's evening...

1 lb. butternut squash (small cubed)
1 onion (chopped)
1 packet quick-cook risotto rice
Olive oil
Water as per packet instructions
1 glass white wine
2 pinches mixed herbs

Fry the squash in a little olive oil for 10 minutes or until just tender, adding the herbs towards the end of the cooking time. Add the onion and fry for 5 more minutes until soft. Add the wine and simmer until evaporated, then add the rice and water. Cook until all the liquid has been absorbed and the rice is tender. Serve with a colourful salad.

Morning Dew Breakfast

There is no better way to start the day than with a cooked breakfast, a glorious view and plenty of refreshing morning dew on the ground...

4 rashers bacon (thick slices)	**2 thick slices black pudding**
2 large tomatoes (halved)	**3 free range eggs**
2 large mushrooms	**Tomato sauce**

Fry the rashers of bacon and black pudding on the BBQ until almost cooked, add the mushrooms and tomatoes and cook until brown. Meanwhile, fry the eggs on the stove in the van. Serve with lashings of tomato sauce and a large mug of Camper Van tea.

Toasty Eggy Bread

What better way to wake up in the morning – apart from some beautiful sunshine, of course...

4 free range eggs   **4 slices bread**
A little milk (around half a cup full)   **Oil to fry**

Break all the eggs into a bowl and whisk in a little milk to form a thick eggy batter. Dip the bread into the mixture and fry in a hot frying pan for a few seconds until brown on both sides. Serve with lashings of piping hot baked beans.

Strawberry Fair Mousse

If your Camper Van has a fridge, then clear the beers out for just a few hours...

5 oz. Strawberries (chopped but save 2 for garnish)
Sugar (a good sprinkle)
Handful marshmallows
3 fl. oz. double cream (whipped) (reserve any remaining cream to serve).
1 fl. oz. water

Gently heat the strawberries and water for 2 or 3 minutes, then remove from the heat and mash. Add the marshmallows and gently heat until they have dissolved. Allow to cool, then fold in the whipped cream and place in the camper van fridge for a few hours until set. Serve with any remaining cream and strawberries.

Summer Holiday Pudding

A summer pudding you can make anytime of the year...

1 can summer fruits
1 small punnet of strawberries (chopped but reserve a few to garnish)
Sugar
4 slices white bread, crusts removed
Ice cream squirt sauce (strawberry works well)
Double cream (to serve)

Lightly oil 2 mugs and line with cling film. Mix together the tinned fruit (and half the juice), fresh strawberries and sugar. Cut the bread to form a small circle for the base of the mugs, slices for the sides and a larger circle for the lid. Spread the ice cream sauce on one side of the bread and place in the mould, sauce side against the mould. Fill the centre with the fruit mixture and press down well, topping with the lid. Tap the pudding from the mugs and place on a plate. Serve with lashings of cream, the remaining juice and the reserved strawberries.

Craggy Cranachan

If motoring around Scotland, then this is a must...

1½ oz. oats, toasted
2 fl. oz. double cream, whipped
Greek yoghurt (small tub)

2 oz. raspberries (save some for the garnish)
2 tbsp Scottish Heather Honey
Serve with Scottish Shortbread

Toast the oats in the grill or in a dry frying pan for a few moments. Then simply place all the ingredients into a bowl and mix together. Serve with a whole raspberry on top and with some delicious Scottish Shortbread on the side.

Off-Road Tiramisu

This is so easy to make in a Camper Van, especially for that special occasion...

4 fl. oz. coffee	3 fl. oz. double cream (whipped)
8 sponge fingers	2 oz. pecans, chopped
$^1/_2$ orange (juice only)	3 oz. raspberries
3 oz. cream cheese	4 chunks dark chocolate (grated)

Pour the coffee into a bowl and soak the sponge fingers in the coffee. Place the sponge fingers into the base of a glass dish. In a bowl, mix together the orange juice, cream cheese and double cream until well combined. Next, fold in the raspberries and pecans.

Spread the cream mixture over the sponge fingers and sprinkle over the grated chocolate. Serve immediately with any spare cream on the side.

Sunny Ice Cream with Hot Cherry Sauce

Just the thought is enough to make you stop at the next ice cream parlour...

1 oz. caster sugar
Can of cherries (pie filling works well)
Slug red wine

Gently heat the sugar and cherry juice until dissolved. Add the red wine, bring to the boil and simmer until reduced and the sauce has thickened. Fold in the cherries and warm through. Serve over a large chunk of locally made ice cream.

Good Night...

Zzzzzzzzzzzz.........

12 oz. boiling water   **4 tbsp clear honey**
Mini bottle of whisky   **½ lemon, juice only**

Place all the ingredients into a small jug and stir. Allow to cool slightly, then serve...

METRIC CONVERSIONS

The weights, measures and oven temperatures used in the preceding recipes can be easily converted to their metric equivalents. The conversions listed below are only approximate, having been rounded up or down as may be appropriate.

Weights

Avoirdupois	Metric
1 oz.	just under 30 grams
4 oz. (¼ lb.)	app. 115 grams
8 oz. (½ lb.)	app. 230 grams
1 lb.	454 grams

Liquid Measures

Imperial	Metric
1 tablespoon (liquid only)	20 millilitres
1 fl. oz.	app. 30 millilitres
1 gill (¼ pt.)	app. 145 millilitres
½ pt.	app. 285 millilitres
1 pt.	app. 570 millilitres
1 qt.	app. 1.140 litres

Oven Temperatures

	°Fahrenheit	Gas Mark	°Celsius
Slow	300	2	150
	325	3	170
Moderate	350	4	180
	375	5	190
	400	6	200
Hot	425	7	220
	450	8	230
	475	9	240

Flour as specified in these recipes refers to plain flour unless otherwise described.